DIRECTIONS

by

Jeff MacNelly

With a foreword by Jack Fuller
editorial page editor, *Chicago Tribune*

Andrews, McMeel & Parker Inc.
A Universal Press Syndicate Company
Kansas City ● New York

ISBN: 0-8362-1220-7
Library of Congress Catalog Number: 83-073614

┌─ *ATTENTION: SCHOOLS AND BUSINESSES* ─────────┐

Andrews, McMeel & Parker books are available at quantity discounts with bulk purchase for educational, business, or sales promotional use. For information, please write to: Special Sales Department, Andrews, McMeel & Parker Inc., 4400 Johnson Drive, Fairway, Kansas 66205.

└──┘

Foreword

You are about to encounter one of the finest, strangest minds in the newspaper business. He is Jeff MacNelly. He draws political cartoons.

Sometimes, when I feel like boasting, I tell people that I am Jeff MacNelly's editor. Don't believe it. Nothing is further from the truth. You do not edit a political cartoonist's work. You learn not to suggest ideas you think are funny. He's got his own. Sure, maybe you sit down periodically and talk things over — the weather, the World Series, important things — the way a barber might. But then you simply wait with fingers crossed for the latest cartoon to arrive. And when Jeff ambles in with it and everyone gathers around for a look and passes Xerox copies from office to office, you sit back and congratulate yourself for all your hard work.

At the *Chicago Tribune,* Jeff has an office high in Tribune Tower. His digs are so remote that to get to the editorial board meetings, he has to change elevators twice. He probably thinks of this as commuting, and if you asked him I'm sure he would tell you that the distance is just about right.

I do not know exactly what he does way up there, but he assures me that the view is fine. It reminds me of a story they tell about Col. Robert R. McCormick, once the publisher of the *Tribune,* who also made his place in the sky. One day, late in McCormick's career, a reporter from another publication was interviewing the colonel for a profile. The reporter asked him why a man who owned big, powerful newspapers in New York and, at that time, in Washington, D.C., had chosen to keep his headquarters in Chicago. The colonel went over to the panoramic window and gazed downward. "Son," he said, "I sit up here every day on this ledge with a bunch of roses in one hand and a handful of night soil in the other, and eventually *everybody* passes under my window."

Jeff is a dispenser of roses and night soil, too. And truth to tell, he's pretty stingy with the roses. His cartoons are magic. They make us laugh, and sometimes we laugh most heartily when the joke is on our own most precious ideas. I wish I could say just what combination of graphic mastery, writing skill, and sheer perversity goes into Jeff's work. I can't, but there are a few things I know for sure.

The guy draws like a dream. When you look at these cartoons you will see an extraordinary eye at work. It is not only that the caricatures are right on the money, showing more than how people look, showing who they *are.* It is not only the detail, the embellishments, that keep you looking as you laugh. When people say Jeff has a special perspective on the world, they are engaging in heroic understatement. He sees things from a point of view where the images are powerful and everything is clear. He is a lucky man.

Another thing I know is that Jeff is a better writer than most people who make their living by words alone. It took a long time for me to recognize this, probably because I hated to admit that somebody who drew so well could be so good at the thing that I do, too. Jeff has a knack for capturing the essence of human speech and putting it into a little bubble over a figure's head. He is a master at mimicry and parody. It is hard today to hear Al Haig or Jimmy Carter or Teddy Kennedy or Jesse Jackson speak and not measure them against Jeff's version. Poor guys.

When I went through the cartoons in this book, I had seen all of them before. But damned if I didn't laugh again when I saw them. And I'm sure you will too. Unless, perhaps, you're Al Haig or Ted Kennedy or Jimmy Carter. . . .

— Jack Fuller, editorial page editor, *Chicago Tribune*

Introduction

A few words before we get to the pictures.

People always ask cartoonists where it is that we get our ideas. It's easy: We have the greatest gag writers in the world working for us up in Washington. When I sit down to do one of these it's more of an editing problem than it is a purely creative task. The cartoon characters are already in place, there are a dozen different plots kicking around, and the dialogue is usually hilarious. The American people obviously have a great affection for cartoonists. They demonstrate this every election when they deliver us victims that are consistently silly, gloriously funny-looking, and capable of the most bizarre behavior. Which is to say they can always be counted on to elect folks that represent a very accurate cross section of our nation.

In fact, it is always a challenge for me to come up with something in my cartoons that is more fantastic than reality itself. On the days that I am working on *Shoe* I usually find it much harder to come up with material because I created the birds and their world. They exist within the increasingly cramped confines of my skull and are therefore subjected to and influenced by a certain degree of rationality, a few ounces of intelligence, and about a teaspoonful of organization that rattles around in there with them. The *real* world never has to operate under those constraints.

One thing to remember when you go through this collection: Political cartooning is a negative art. We rarely say anything nice in our cartoons. Our main weapon is ridicule which, if it's going to be effective, should be used with the finesse and charm of a twelve gauge. Our favorite targets are those who take themselves seriously and have no sense of humor or perspective. We are supposedly journalists yet no reporter could get away with what we do in our space in the newspaper. We stretch the facts, we misquote, we take everything out of context and tiptoe along the borderline of slander. Yet, after the smoke clears, we have probably gotten closer to the truth than our colleagues in the news columns who have to try to stick to the rules.

— Jeff MacNelly

The Endless Campaign

13

Good grief! The Archbishop's been MIRVed.

15

17

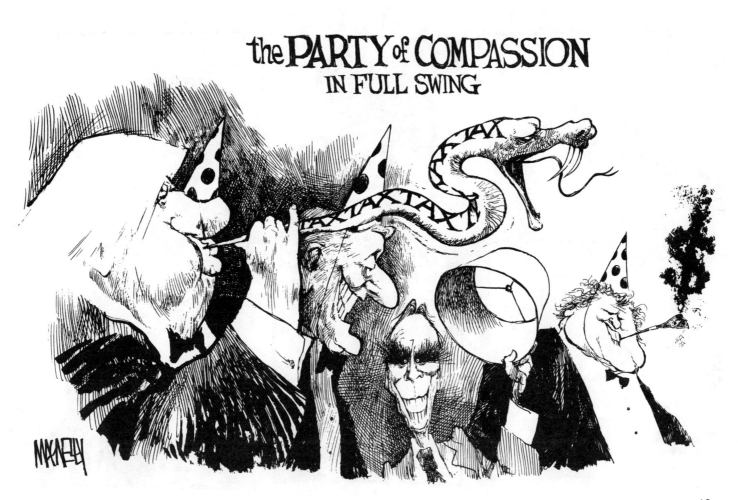

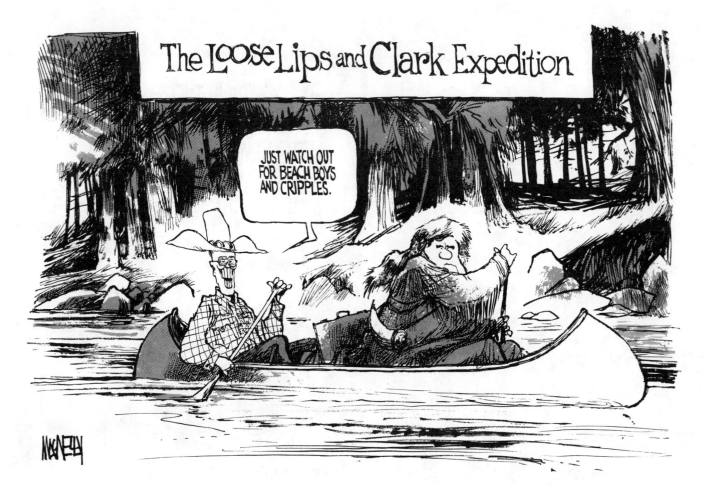

Return of the Jimmy – STAR WARS '84

MacNelly

Darth Mondale

Glenn Skywalker

Cranston Threepio

Askew D2

Wookie Hart

and Ted Solo

24

Fritz Mondale and the Carter endorsement.

The Carter Legacy

28

31

32

33

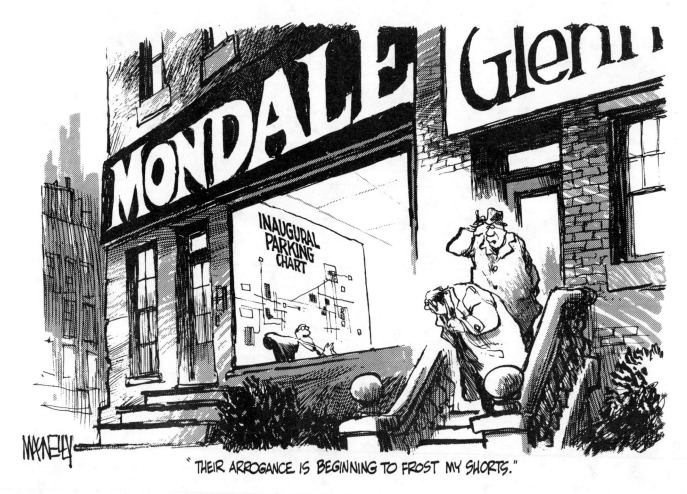

"THEIR ARROGANCE IS BEGINNING TO FROST MY SHORTS."

41

The Russians

HEROES OF SOVIET AGRICULTURE

45

50

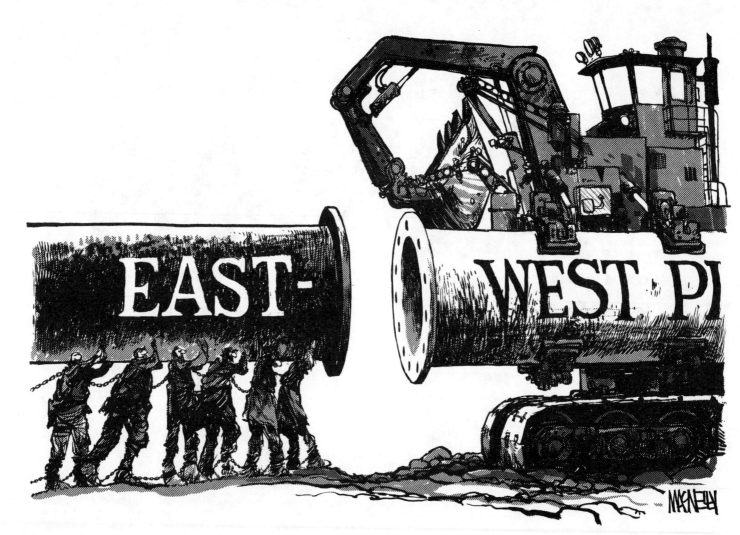

61

OFFICIAL SOVIET ENEMY AIRCRAFT SILHOUETTE CHART

MacNELLY

U·2 SPYPLANE

B·1 BOMBER

U.S. NAVY F·14

STEALTH BOMBER

CRUISE MISSILE

82 ND AIRBORNE.

F·4 PHANTOM

"We are surrounded by dangerous paranoids, Comrade. — Call in an air strike!!"

64

66

67

Amerinomics

1. 2
−3
= depending on outyear actuarial projections and then assuming revenue enhancement combined with a modest adjustment in the retirement age if
POLITICS
83
THIS IS NOT AN ESSAY QUESTION, BOZO!
Social Security MATH TEST
MACNELLY

79

89

"You're WHAT?"

92

Trouble Spots

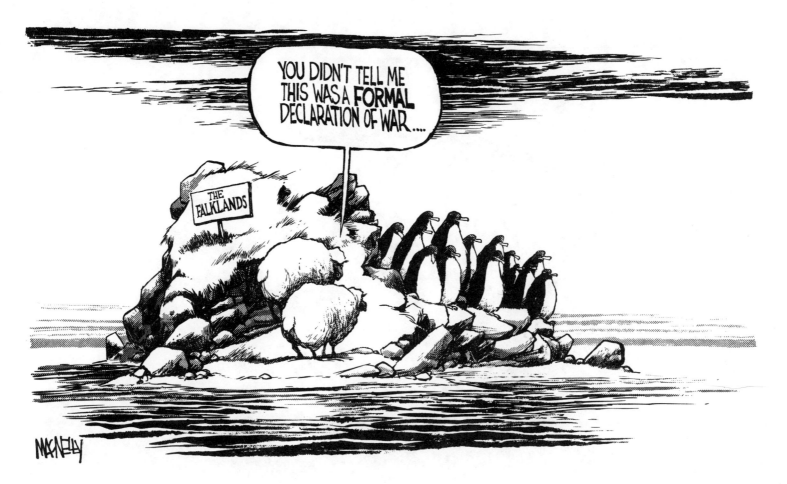

98

99

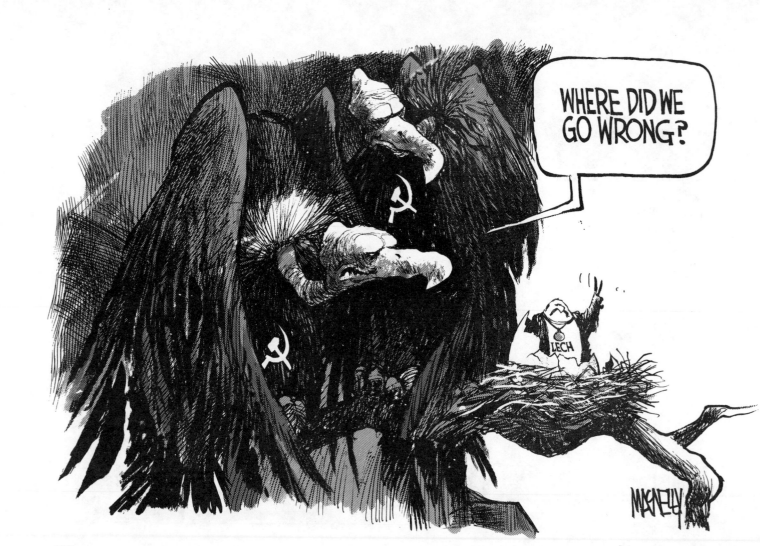

100

106

Mine Detector

107

107

109

111

113

114

118

The Years with Jimmy

HI THERE!

I'M JIMMY CARTER...

AND I NEED YOUR HELP.

A VERY SPECIAL KIND OF HELP.

YOU SEE, FOR THE PAST YEAR...

...I'VE HAD THIS COAT HANGER STUCK IN MY MOUTH.....

129

130

131

132

133

135

137

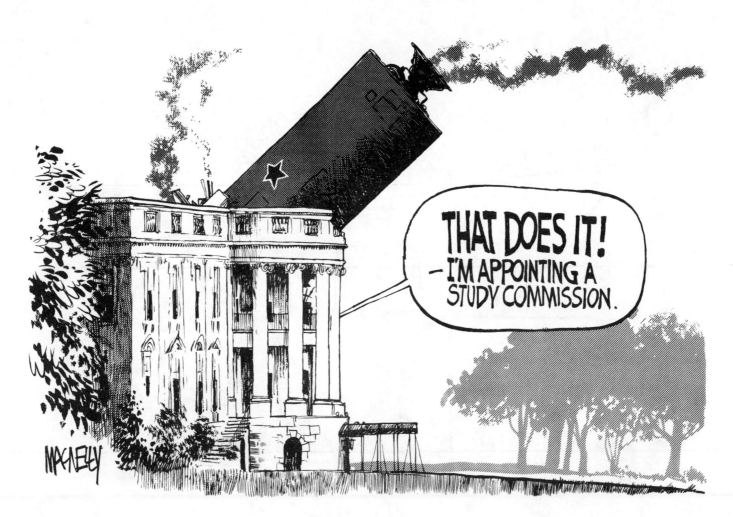

138

143

147

148

149

Oldies

'GO FISH.'

'"JOHN DEAN IN CONCERT AT THE WHITE HOUSE?" "LET'S SEE ... WOULD THAT BE UNDER "BLUES" OR "HARD ROCK"?'

`'"GOODNESS GRACIOUS!" CRIED DICK. "THE TAPES! THEY'VE DISAPPEARED!"...'`

' WELL, THERE I WAS, PLAYING "HAIL TO THE CHIEF" ON WHAT I <u>THOUGHT</u> WAS MY ACCORDION...'

'YES, A SMALL CONCESSION PERHAPS, BUT I DOUBT IF ANYBODY WILL REALLY MISS NEW JERSEY...'

'YOU FELLERS WON'T BELIEVE THIS, BUT I WAS ONCE CONSIDERED PRESIDENTIAL MATERIAL...
BEFORE I STARTED HITTIN' THE BOTTLE, THAT IS ....'

GUMS

"LET ME KNOW IF YOU HEAR ANYTHING SUSPICIOUS."

"IT'S FROM TANIA.... SHE'S CHANGED HER NAME TO PATTY AND JOINED THE FBI."

THE UNDECIDED VOTER

March 11, 1977

Form **1040**

US Department of the Treasury – INTERNAL REVENUE SERVICE
Individual Income Tax Return

1976

FOR THE YEAR JANUARY 1 – DECEMBER 31, 1976, OR WHENEVER YOU GET AROUND TO IT

Please Type or Print

Name **JEFF ~~MacNELLY~~**   Last Name **MACNELLY**   Second-to-Last Initial   STARCH? ☐ Yes ☐ No ☒

☐ CUFFS   ☐ NO CUFFS

FOR IRS USE ONLY

Present Address of Addressee (must be filled out by Addressor or legal Guardian of Aforementioned (unless greater than Line B above)
The RICHMOND NEWS Leader

City, Town, Post office, SHOE SIZE (NO 12½)   IS YOUR ADDRESS GREATER THAN LINE 41? ☐ NO   IF YES, WHY? ☐ YES   OCC-U-PATION ► YOURS _____ ► SPOUSE _____

YOU ARE Here ☐ yes ☐ No

REQUESTED BY DEPARTMENT OF AGRICULTURE. ► A. HOW MANY TALKING CHICKENS DO YOU OWN? 0. | B. NAMES C. DO ANY OF THEM PLAY THE OBOE? ☐ yes ☐ No | DO YOU LIVE WITHIN 2 MILES OF A DECENT PIZZA PLACE? ☐ Yes ☐ No ☐ EXTRA CHEESE | D. Have you Rotated your Tires Lately? ☐ Yes ☐ No | IF NO, FILE IRS Tire Rotation Schedule L | E. YES? ☐ NO F. NO? ☐ YES

Filing Status

1 ☐ Single   ☐ Double   ☐ Sacrifice Fly
2 ☐ Married Filing Singly joint return (even IF SPOUSE IS MARRIED SEPARATELY)
3 ☐ Joint married singly separate spouse (but FILING DOUBLE JOINTED)
4 ☐ Head of Household filing separate but joint return (if UNMARRIED BUT JOINTLY SINGLE)
5 ☐ Head of joint filing single file spouse's separately
6 ☐ Widow(er) with separate dependent filing out of joint return singly

Exemptions

41 a REGULAR? ☐ yourself? ☐ Spouse ☐
b Names of Dependent children who lived with you _____ Why? _____
c Just First names, Dummy. . . . .
4. Do you weigh more than last year's tax form?
e Number of Parakeets subtracted from Gross Rotated Income (PLUS Line 27 – UNLESS GREATER THAN TWELVE MILES) . . . .
f How many inches in a liter? _____
7 a Total Confusion (add lines 6e AND f, g; fold in eggs, beat until firm). . . ►

ENTER NUMBER OF BOXES CHECKED ►
CHECK NUMBER OF BOXES ENTERED ►
ENTER NUMBER OF CHECKERED BOXERS ►
DO NOTHING Here ►

8 Presidential Election Campaign Fund . . ► DO YOU WISH TO DESIGNATE $1 OF YOUR TAXES TO THIS WORTHY CAUSE? . . . . ☐ Yes ☐ No | ISN'T THIS A DUMB LAW? ☐ Yes ☐ No | WHAT ABOUT THE LITTLE LADY? | NOTE: IF YOU CHECKED Yes WE WILL COME AND STEAL ALL YOUR HUBCAPS

9 Wages, Salaries, Tips, Extortion ◄ ATTACH W2 FORMS TO YOUR FOREHEAD ► WITH HEAVY DUTY STAPLE GUN . . . . ► | 9.
10 Remunerations . . . [IF LESS THAN GROSS REIMBURSEMENTS, THEN FILE SCHEDULE Q (See Page 14 of "Joy of Cooking")] | 10.
11 Gross Influx . . . . . | 11.
12 Money you made . . [IF $400 OR LESS, MORE OR LESS, LIST SCHEDULE B WITHOUT NOT FILLING IN PART II AND R2. BUT MORE THAN LINE 8] | 12
13 What about all that cash you stashed in that jar under the garage? | 14. SUBTRACT 13 FROM 14 . . .   15. (THE ANSWER TO 14 IS . . . . 1)

Think of a number between 1 and 10

• HOW WOULD YOU LIKE A GOOD SOCK IN THE FACE, FELLA? ☐ Yes ☐ No
• IF LINE 15 IS BIGGER THAN A BREADBOX OR MORE, GO TO LINE 43 TO FIGURE TAX

TAX RATE SCHEDULE X, Y, OR 12 ☐ See Page 7 of INSTRUCTIONS CHECK HERE ►

← here   ← or here